A
Tataviam
Creation
Story

Enjoy!!

A Tataviam Creation Story

by

Alan Salazar
"Puchuk Ya'ia'c"

FERNANDEÑO TATAVIAM STORYTELLER

with Illustrations by

Mona Lewis

Sunsprite

Publications

We would like to acknowledge the many people who helped bring this story to life.
Thank you Jazmin Aminian Jordán, your encouragement and support have been invaluable!
Thanks also go to tribal members Beverly Folkes, Dennis Garcia, Kathy Ann Flores
and Bernice Cooke for your kind support and beautiful images for our book. We thank
Raymond Braveowl for the beautiful translations into the Tataviam/Serrano language
and for his tireless work on behalf of the Tataviam Tribe in the recovery of our
original dialect. With deep appreciation, we thank John R. Johnson, Ph.D., Curator
of Anthropology at the Santa Barbara Museum of Natural History for your work
researching the history of our tribe and for sharing your treasure-trove of information
so generously with us. We gratefully acknowledge Rudy Ortega, the Tataviam Band
of Mission Indians Tribal President, and Kimia Fatehi, the tribe's Chief of Staff for
their support and the sharing of their vast knowledge of tribal history.

Published by Sunsprite Publications
Ventura, California

Copy Editing by Andra Vltavín
Design and Typesetting by Ash Good

ISBN-13 (Paperback): 978-1-7358195-4-9
ISBN-1 (Hardcover): 978-1-7358195-5-6
Library of Congress Control Number: 2021920356

TO MY DAUGHTER. MELISSA: MY SON. ERIC;
AND MY GRANDSON. CADEN. my stories are for you.
Having you three help with painting was so special.
I hope I inspire you and all future storytellers
to write your own stories. We are all storytellers,
so practice your craft.
Melissa, Eric, and Caden, I love you.

—DAD/PAPAW

FOR MY DAUGHTERS. who are my inspiration.
AND FOR THE CHILDREN. who still hear the stories
of the land, and hold all its inhabitants
with tender hands and tender hearts.

—ML

Contents

A Tataviam Creation Story

The Tataviam are a small California
tribe from northern Los Angeles County.
"Tataviam" means "people facing the sun."
It is what our neighbors to the north,
the Kitenemuk tribe, called us. We, the
Tataviam people, believe we have lived in
Tataviam territory since time immemorial.
The Santa Clarita Valley is the center of
Tataviam territory—it is our heart.

In order for tribal cultures to survive, we
must sing new songs and tell new stories.
This is my original creation story. I tell it in
the spirit of my Tataviam ancestors.

—Alan Salazar "Puchuk Ya'ia'c"

A FEW WORDS IN
THE Tataviam LANGUAGE

"The Tataviam had clans."

Tataaiamvuˈ kiikichawanqam qac.

PHONETICALLY:

tah-tah-vee-ah-voo kee-kee-cha-wahn-kahm kach

"The animals were our teachers."

Yeiiyeiinammuˈ chenyuˈ
nahtavuniniam.

yay-yay-nah-moo chen-yoo nah-tav-ooh-nee-nee-yum

"The animals gathered,
and they made the people."

Yeiiyeiinammuˈ piyumˈk
kwenemuˈ taaqtami ichuˈkin.

*yay-yay-nah-moo pee-yoomk
kwe-neh-moo tak-tah-mee ee-choo-kin*

Santa Clarita Valley   ○ Ancient Village   ● Modern City

Castaic
Lake

Piinga

Piru

Ventura   SANTA CLARA RIVER   Coaynga   Chaguaynga   Newhall

This story happens near the ancient village of Chaguayanga along the shores of the Santa Clara River where my Tataviam ancestors lived. I tell this story in the spirit of traditional Tataviam myth and legend. Many of our stories have been lost. I have researched how my tribe lived and what they believed to guide this story. The Tataviam are a clan-based people. We look to the animals as teachers. We have the bear clan, eagle clan, turtle clan, and coyote clan, to name a few.

Tribal creation stories are very important. This one defines who the Tataviam people are, and tells how the animals we respect created the Tataviam people.

Long, long ago,

there were no people living in Tataviam territory. For thousands and thousands of years, only the animals and plants lived in Tataviam territory.

In those days, the animals had a great council, the Tataviam Council of Animals. This council consisted of Bear, Eagle, Deer, Lizard, Turtle, Raven, Spider, and Coyote.

It was the first meeting of the year— the first day of spring. The council met at a sacred cave in the mountains just north of the Santa Clara River. It is known today as Bower Cave.

Bear had just awakened from his winter sleep. During his hibernation, he had had a dream. He dreamed of a new creature that stood and walked on two legs. Bear had heard from his cousins who lived way up north that there were creatures the polar bears called people. Bear knew he was dreaming of the Tataviam people. Bear called the council of animals together to decide what the Tataviam people would look like and how they would survive.

Each member of the council wanted the Tataviam people to look like them. Coyote was especially proud of his appearance. He thought his eyes, his ears, and even his tail would look great on the Tataviam people. Coyote argued with all the other animals about every little thing. This great debate went on and on and on . . .

Eagle said, "Since the Tataviam people will stand on two legs, their feet are very important."

Coyote naturally suggested paws for the Tataviam's feet.

Spider said, "Maybe the Tataviam should have four feet and four hands."

All the animals said, "NO!!!" at the same time.

But Eagle knew who had the best feet.
Eagle asked Bear to show everyone his feet.
When the others saw Bear's feet, they all
agreed the Tataviam should have feet like
Bear. Well, everyone except Coyote.

Coyote said. "The Tataviam people should have yellow eyes like mine."

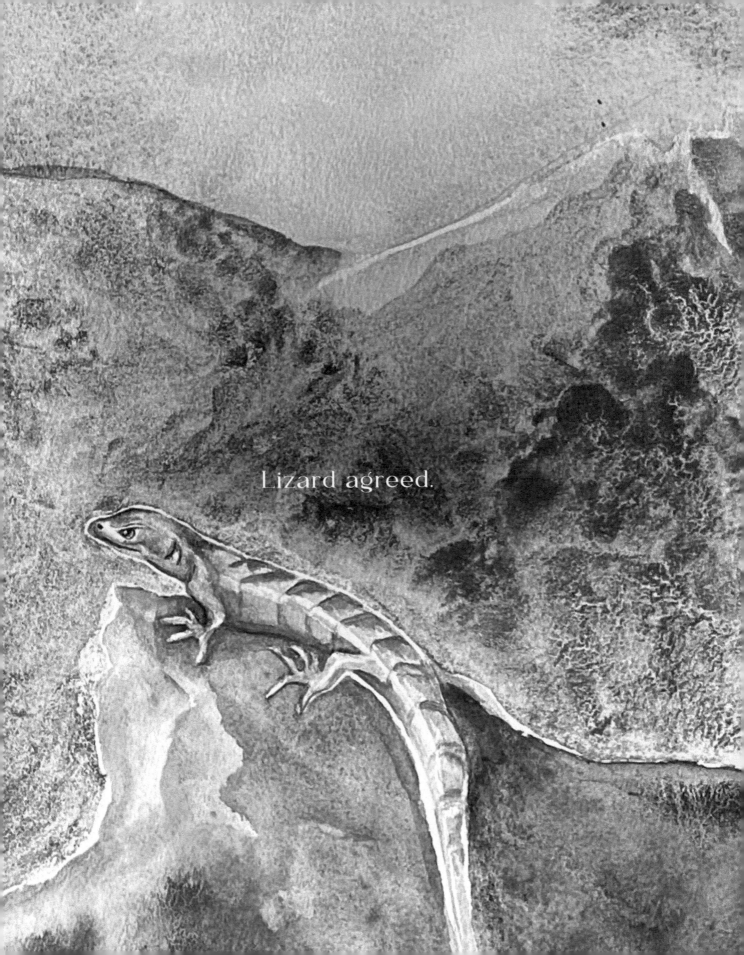

Lizard agreed.

But all the other animals thought
brown eyes like Deer's were better.
Well, everyone except Coyote.

Then Coyote said, "The Tataviam
people should have a tail like mine."

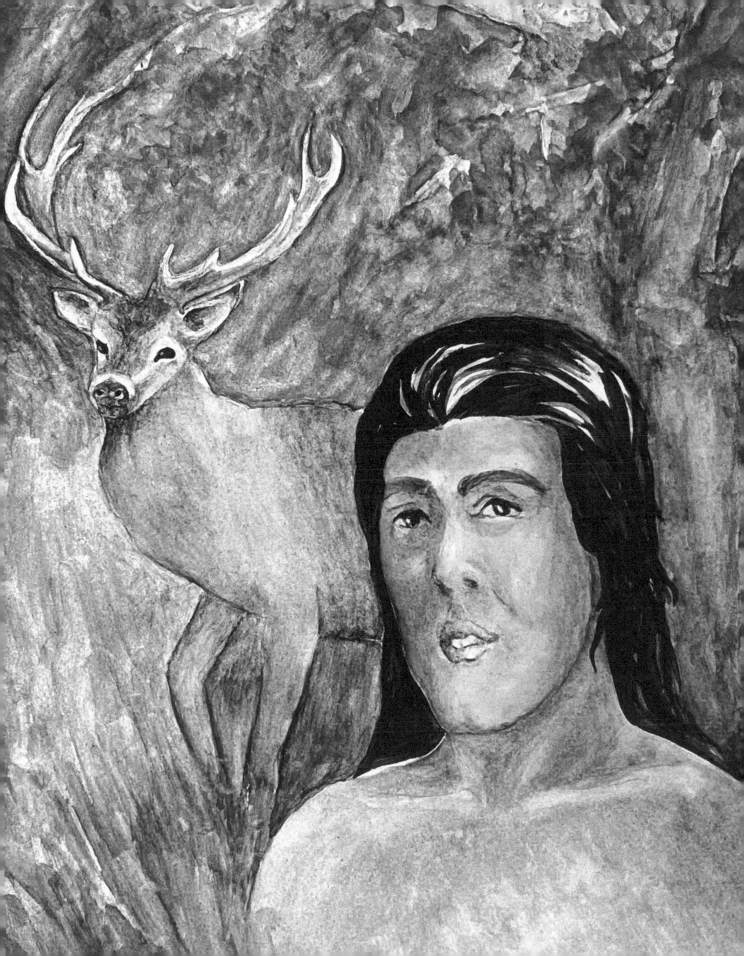

Turtle said, "Noooooo, a tail like miiiiiinnnne."

Bear stood up and said, "No, the Tataviam people should not have any tail. We have to keep some things so we will be special."

All the animals agreed. Well, everyone except Coyote.

Then Turtle stood up as tall as she could and said, "Whaaaaaat about color?"

Coyote jumped up and said, "The Tataviam people should be a little grayish, a little reddish, a little tan, maybe some beige with a little white and black scattered about."

Turtle said, "Sooooo Coyote, you want them to have your colors? I think theeeeeey should beeeee just one color."

Turtle sloooowly looked at all the animals veeeeeeeery carefully, slooooowly checking everyone's fur, feathers, and scales. Turtle looked at everything—the plants, the sky, and the ground they all stood on.

After a moment of thought, Turtle said, "The brown color of Mother Earth is so beautiful. I think the Tataviam should be brown. We all come from Mother Earth and so do the Tataviam people."

All the animals agreed. Well, everyone except Coyote.

After several days and several nights, the Tataviam Council of Animals had decided on everything about the Tataviam people. The animals were all very happy. Well, everyone except Coyote.

Deer said, "Our work is done. May we go home?"

But Raven CAWED!!! and CAWED!!!!
as loud as he could to get everyone's
attention.

Raven, who had sat quietly during the
whole meeting said, "The Tataviam
people should also have something
else from all the animals."

Bear, with a confused look, said,
"What are you talking about Raven?
We have decided on everything about
the Tataviam people."

Raven CAWED!!! and CAWED!!!! again really loud and said, "All of us have our own gift, our own power, our own spirit. We are all teachers. We teach our young how to survive. We teach how to hunt in a good way. We teach how to gather plants in a respectful way. We teach which plants are for food and which are for medicine.

I think the Tataviam people should have the gifts, the powers, and the spirits of us. Some of the Tataviam will have Raven spirit, some will have Bear spirit, some Eagle spirit, some Lizard spirit, some Turtle spirit, some Deer spirit, some Spider spirit, and most importantly, some will have Coyote spirit."

Raven continued, "The Tataviam people will be fast, slow, tall, short, fierce, timid, hardworking, intelligent, beautiful, playful, strong, and clever."

"Clever like me, dude?" asked Coyote (it was Coyote who started the "dude" thing).

"Yes, clever like you, Coyote," said Raven.

All the animals agreed, even Coyote.

Now you know who created the
Tataviam people and why we still
respect all the animals. They are
teachers, and we can learn from
all of them.

Every one of us has our own gift,
our own power, and our own spirit.
We are all connected to Mother Earth.

We all need each other to survive.
Some believe that the first Tataviam
people were over 20 feet tall, but that
is another story for another day.

I encourage you to go for a hike
out in nature, sit under the shade
of a tree and watch all the animals.
Maybe you will learn something
about the animals and about yourself.
The Tataviam have done this for
thousands of years.

the end

Animal Teachers

Many tribal cultures all around the world see animals as teachers. The Tataviam have studied the animals for thousands of years. We believe we can learn many important lessons from the animals we live with. They are our neighbors. We share the resources that Mother Earth has blessed us with. We need them more than they need us. So, the Tataviam believe that we should respect all the animals, big and small. Some of the animals we hunt, but we still honor them. Some of the animals we just admire. We try to respect both. The animals that we use as teachers are as unique as the teachers in every classroom across America. For instance, some teachers teach us how to sing—choir teachers. Birds can also teach us how to sing. Whales also sing beautiful songs. Or we can think of the woodworking teacher who teaches us how to build things, reminding us of the beaver that builds incredible dams. I believe that everyone is a teacher. We should all take the time to learn from our neighbors, friends, and family members. Grandmas, grandpas, aunties, uncles, cousins, nieces, and nephews are all teachers. We can learn many things from each of them. Here are just a few of the animals that the Tataviam look to as teachers.

Bear

Bears are very respected because they are the biggest and strongest animals in Tataviam territory. Today, we believe that Bear has healing power. I believe that when you are sick, you are weak. You might have the flu, which makes you have a temperature, and you have no energy. You just want to curl up under a blanket and sleep. So, if you are sick and weak, visualize a big, strong Bear—just awakened from hibernation. Bear is also a great fisherman and a strong swimmer. For such a large animal, Bear can run very fast. Even if you are a large human, you may still need to run fast on occasion. Finally, we are like Bear in our eating habits. The Tataviam people and bears both eat meat and plants; we are both omnivores. If you study bears, you will find that many things they eat are things you can also eat, such as wild berries.

Spider

Spider is also a very important teacher. Many of the small creatures are sometimes forgotten. As Americans, we are impressed with big, strong, and powerful animals. Or, we love the cute little animals. Baby cottontail rabbits and baby quail are really cute. But, spiders are very important teachers. Their homes are works of art.

Every spiderweb is unique. Spider very carefully weaves a web, then patiently waits for dinner to get caught in that sticky web. Those fine silky threads of a spiderweb are some of the strongest known fibers. Spiderweb fibers are said to be five times stronger than steel at the same diameter. Some spiders can jump 50 times their body length. So, if you are a basketball player or broad jumper in track and field, you might want Spider spirit to help you jump. Yes, some are poisonous, so be careful. But, if we watch spiders, we can learn many things.

Golden Eagle

Golden Eagle is one of the most respected animals in many tribal cultures. They fly higher than any bird. We believe they can take our prayers to the upper world or, as the Greeks believed, to the gods. They are great hunters. Their vision is far superior to ours. When they tuck their wings to dive down on their prey, they reach speeds of more than 150 miles per hour. In the animal world, they live long lives, 30 years on average and 50 years in captivity. Husband and wife golden eagles will hunt as a team. They stay together as husband and wife for life. So, the Tataviam have regarded the golden eagle as a teacher for many reasons.

Coyote

Coyote is very intelligent, but he can also be very silly. He is like a politician; he will say and do whatever it takes to survive. He will not always be very honest, unless being honest will help him. Coyotes are very social but also often like to be by themselves. They are great long-distance runners and can chase a deer for miles and miles until the deer becomes exhausted and easy to take down. They will eat just about anything. They have been seen catching fish as a team. One coyote will scare the fish downstream to a quiet pool area where another coyote is patiently waiting. The coyote that catches the fish with her mouth always throws one or two on the nearby shore for her mate. In the Tataviam culture, Coyote is not seen as a trickster. Coyote is respected for being smart, clever, mischievous, silly, social, and independent, much like us humans.

These are just some of the many lessons we can learn from our animal neighbors. I encourage everyone to watch, observe, and listen to Raven, Turtle, Coyote, Deer, Lizard, and all our wild animal neighbors. I enjoy listening to all the birds whistling, chirping, and cawing—it makes me happy. I try my best to whistle, chirp, and caw back to them. Maybe we can learn how to be wild like them.

Now, onto Tataviam tribal history.

The
Tataviam
History

This is the Tataviam history as I know it. Before
European settlers arrived in this area, the tribal villages in Los Angeles
County were independent from one another. This meant that each
village had its own leader, rules, and economy. The group of indigenous
villages in the Santa Clarita Valley and its surrounding mountain ranges
is known collectively as "Tataviam." The Tataviam mostly inhabited the
south-facing slopes of the local mountains, which is how we received
the name "Tataviam" from the Kitanemuk people. Tataviam translates to
"the people facing the sun."

Most tribes have creation stories that describe how they came to be and
who created them. These stories pass down orally from one generation
to the next. We, the Tataviam, have lived in our homelands for thousands
of years. Some anthropologists, people who study cultures, believe
the Tataviam might have moved from the Mojave Desert to the Santa
Clarita Valley about 3,000 years ago. That is just one theory. We, the

Tataviam people, know that we have lived here much longer—
since time immemorial. This place—Tataveaveat—is our home.
This is where we were created. Regardless of how many theories
there are about a tribe's existence, we believe it is most important
to listen to the tribal communities themselves.

Anthropologists have labeled us "hunters and gatherers." We, the
Tataviam, know that our ancestors were much more than hunters
and gatherers. We were also business people who traded with
neighboring tribal groups such as the Chumash, Yuhaviatam, and
Kitanemuk. The Tataviam had an abundance of natural resources
and plenty of wild game to hunt, more than what was needed to
survive. So, we traded what we had a lot of with our neighboring
tribes for things we did not have. It is called bartering. You trade
deer hides for elk hides, for example.

The Tataviam hunted the tule elk in the San Joaquin Valley, near
modern day Bakersfield. That is Yokut tribal territory, the tribe
indigenous to that area. We needed their permission to hunt in
their territory much like we would need the permission of the
Canadian government to hunt moose in Canada today. We had a
business agreement with the Yokuts and the other neighboring
tribes. We upheld tribal territories through mutual understandings
of respect. If our acorn crop was better than their acorn crop,
we gave them acorn flour. If we collected more pine nuts from the
pinyon pine trees in our mountains than we needed, we traded
them with the Yokut peoples so we could hunt their elk. This is an
example of negotiating; it is what business people do. The Tataviam
people have done this for thousands of years.

Another example is with the Chumash people to the west of the Tataviam. They had shell bead currency and abalone shells, which were both very valuable. We traded those elk hides from the Yokut for the ocean shells from the Chumash, then traded those shells with our neighbors to the east, the Serrano (or Yuhaviatam). The Yuhaviatam people of the Mojave Desert viewed shells from the ocean as valuable. The Yuhaviatam had traded with their neighbors to the north for obsidian, a valuable stone used to make arrowheads. The trading continued on and on. We had business relationships with many tribes in southern California. We bartered from tribe to tribe.

Our trade routes or trails were extensive and went throughout all of California, Nevada, Arizona, and New Mexico. In fact, our trade routes were so useful that they eventually became the locations of freeways today. Many other tribal groups, both large and small in numbers, surround the homeland of the Tataviam. We are in the middle of a complex region of southern California. By having business relationships with neighboring tribes, we were able to survive even though our numbers were small.

The Tataviam were not a war-like people. We had occasional disputes with other tribes, but we were diplomatic. We believed in bartering and negotiating. We would have large gatherings with our neighboring villages that were like outdoor markets. Our villages were small, 100-200 people, so by developing relationships with neighboring villages and neighboring tribes, we formed a mutually beneficial network. We were hunters, gatherers, and business people. We still are; today, we just do our hunting and gathering at Vons and Trader Joe's (*wink*).

Every Tataviam village was like a small city with its own government and leadership. We had a Tomiear, or leader, for every village. Matrilineal villages of Chumash influence had women as leaders, or a Manisar. Members of a village would marry members of another village because it was taboo to marry within your own village or family. This is also how they strengthened economic and trade networks. Each village had spiritual leaders, or Sahovit, a small group of men and women who conducted ceremonies called the Pahavit. The most important ceremonies were the Yamava (spring), Terngava (summer), Chaweyh (fall), and Tamrra (winter) ceremonies. We honored the sun on the shortest day of the year and the longest day of the year. There are many ceremonies the Sahovit were responsible for—naming, puberty, harvest, and burial ceremonies were among them.

During the warm months, the Tataviam did not wear much clothing. Women wore skirts made from thin strips of willow bark or animal hides like rabbit and deer. Men wore a small animal hide similar to a small breechcloth or no materials at all. Men would also wear a skirt of eagle down feathers or thin strips of bark for special ceremonies. During the colder months, both women and men wore animal hide capes wrapped around their bodies, similar to a serape.

Tataviam Traditional Dress

The Tataviam territory covers thousands of acres. It is some of the most beautiful and productive land in California. In the north, we had villages in the mountains near Gorman. We had villages out in the desert near Agua Dulce and Palmdale. Most of our villages are located in the Santa Clarita Valley. It is the heart of our territory. We gave names to places that are still in use today. For example, Piru derives from the Tataviam word Pi'irukng, or place of the grass. These places have thousands of years of stories and memories attached to them.

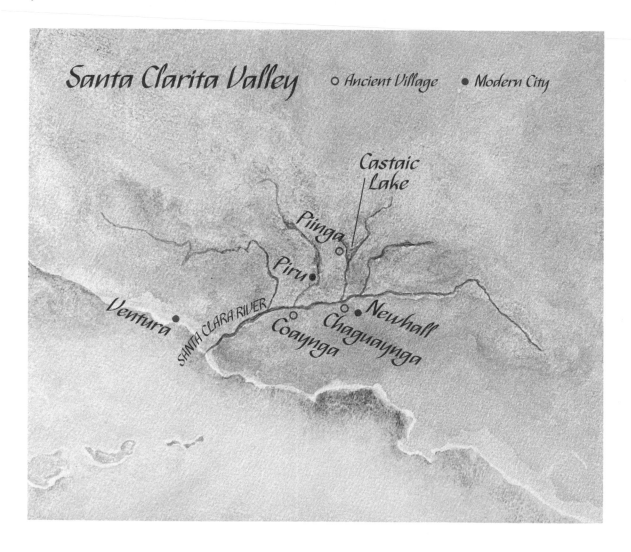

~ 54 ~

Many of our Tataviam villages were along or near the Santa Clara River or other water sources. Before the Spanish, Mexican, and other European people began building dams on our rivers, there were hundreds of creeks and streams in California that flowed with water all year. Those early settlers diverted the water to irrigate crops they were growing. The Tataviam lived near these streams and creeks in the mountains, foothills, and valleys for thousands of years. We had no need to dam the rivers or divert the water from the creeks. We farmed the native plants that grew naturally throughout California. The Tataviam people were very knowledgeable and knew how to manage the resources, both native plants and animals.

Hunting

Thousands of years ago, the Tataviam used spears, traps, and atlatls to hunt animals. The atlatl is a wood shaft with a cup at the end. A hunter would place a spear or dart in the cup and launch it. This allowed hunters to throw their spear or dart over a hundred yards with great accuracy. The spear or dart could reach speeds of over 75 MPH.

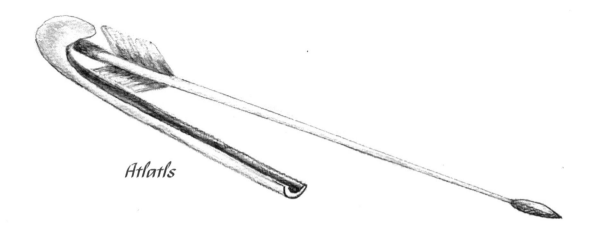

Atlatls

Rabbit Net

The Tataviam used various traps and nets to catch rabbits, quail, ducks, and squirrels. They also used nets and harpoons to catch fish such as rainbow trout, bass, and steelhead trout, to name a few.

Dr. John Johnson, director of the department of anthropology at the museum of Santa Barbara stated that the adaptation of the bow and arrow likely took place around the year AD 500. The bow and arrow allowed us to be even more accurate. Regardless which weapon was used, our hunters were highly skilled. We hunted deer, elk from the Bakersfield area, rabbits, squirrels, ducks, geese, fish, occasionally bears, and even small creatures such as grasshoppers, worms, and slugs.

With any animal we hunted, we only took enough to survive and made sure that we left enough of the animals to hunt the next year. We also shared the plants with the animals to help them survive. Acorns are a good example. The Tataviam people always shared the acorn crop with many animals. We never collected all the acorns. We left enough for the deer, squirrels, blue jays, woodpeckers, and all the animals that ate acorns. They are our neighbors, and they have just as much right to the acorns as the Tataviam people.

As stated earlier, the Tataviam people, like many regional groups, are a clan-based tribe. We look to the animals as teachers. We have the bear clan, the eagle clan, and the lizard clan, to name a few. We studied all the animals. How do they survive? What are their strengths and weaknesses? We can learn many important lessons by just watching a hawk, a coyote, or a towhee bird. Bears eat many of the same things we eat. Bears eat both meat and plants, just like us. Most of the plants they eat, we can eat, too. The Tataviam have known this for a long time. The Tataviam believe we are surrounded by many teachers, both animal and human. If we observe everyone and everything, we can learn many important life lessons. It is a great way to learn—really, just watch the world around you.

Gathering

Before European contact, every Tataviam person knew the names and uses of dozens and dozens of native plants. We knew which plants were poisonous, which ones were edible, and which plants we could use as medicine. When our ancestors were held captive and enslaved at the missions, the Spaniards forbid this knowledge. The young Tataviam people only learned skills that were useful to the missionaries, such as farming and ranching. Our traditional ecological knowledge was not passed down for several generations. Today, our people are recovering from that difficult period. We are reteaching ourselves and our youth this knowledge.

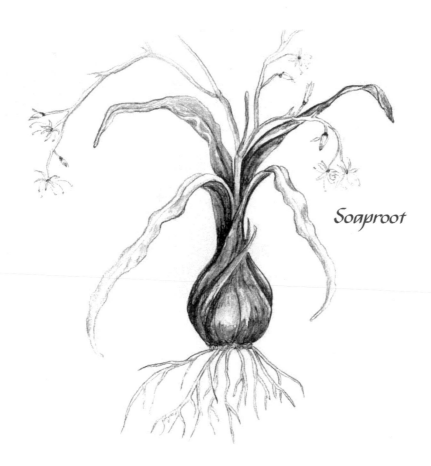

Soaproot

Willow bark helps with pain and headaches. Mugwort helps with rashes and poison oak. Soaproot has many uses; the bulb is edible when cooked. You can also make soap from the bulb and hairbrushes from the fibrous part of the root. The juice from the soaproot bulb causes fish to have difficulty breathing. When someone puts that juice in a pond, the oily juice causes the fish gills to swell, making it difficult to breathe. The fish then swim to the surface to gulp for air, making it easy to harpoon or catch the fish with a net. Elderberry trees are another example of a useful plant. The berries are edible, great in pancakes, and make a very healthy tea. The branches are cut, split, and decorated to make clapper sticks, traditional rhythm instruments that many southern California tribes used. We also made bows for hunting from the elderberry branches.

There are many native plants the Tataviam used. Here are a few: coffee berry, yucca, hummingbird sage, white sage, purple sage, toyon, miner's lettuce, pinyon pine, valley oak trees, coast live oak trees, arroyo willow trees, lemonade berry bush, brodiaeas, mugwort, California wild grape, wild black berries, giant wild rye, juncus, and bulrush tule. There are many more, but I hope you will visit a native nursery or a native garden to learn about our abundance of native plants. Southern California has a very diverse native plant community.

Clapper
Stick
Rattle

Elderberry Tree

Games

The Tataviam played many games. Games of skill were very common. They taught important life skills. Hoop and Spear is one such game of skill. A small 6-12 inch hoop was rolled on the ground. The children took turns throwing their spears through the hoop. If they were more than 50 yards away, it took great skill. Many times, they would be more than 70 yards away. The tribe also played Shinney. Shinney is like field hockey, but our Shinney fields were much larger. The field could be 300 yards by 100 yards or larger with 20-30 players on each team. We also ran races for fun and to develop important life skills. If you were a great runner, or ya'ia'c, you were an important member of the village. We did not have horses; the Spanish brought the horses to California in the 1600s. Walking and running was how we traveled. It was not unusual for our best runners, ya'ia'cs, to run 70-80 miles in a day.

Walnut Dice

We also played games of chance. The walnut dice game was just one of those games. We would take six walnut halves to use as dice. Each player would have colorful sticks about six inches long to bet. If a player threw the dice on the ground and all six dice landed with the flat side up or the rounded side up, they got two sticks from each player. If they threw the dice and they landed three flat up and three rounded up, that was one stick. One, two, four, and five of one type meant no sticks, and you lost your turn. This would go on until one player had everyone's sticks.

Peon was another popular game that many California tribes played, including the Tataviam. Each team of one or two players had a small white stick and a small black stick they held in their hands. The other player or players had to guess which hand the black stick was in. Once again, players won or lost colorful sticks.

Spanish Colonization, Mexican Period, and Early California History

The Spanish came to California in the 1500s and 1600s, staying mostly along the coast. The early explorers were interested in the fur trade and finding places to rest while traveling up and down the California coastline. It was not until the 1760s that colonists established the first Spanish settlements in southern California, mostly forts for the soldiers. The early Spanish explorers brought many diseases as well as cattle, horses, and sheep, which began the destruction of the natural habitat.

The missions brought thousands of Spanish and Mexican settlers to California. The first mission was in San Diego in 1769. They established hundreds of rancherías throughout southern California.

They established the San Fernando Mission in 1797. The damming and diversion of the rivers and creeks for irrigation of crops caused lots of destruction to the natural environment. In order to plant their crops, they removed thousands of oak trees and other native plants from our homelands. This destruction of the native plants along with mass hunting of native animals ruined the Tataviam way of life. The Spanish hunted large animals such as bears, wolves, and mountain lions to near extinction to protect their livestock. As such, Spanish and Mexican settlers destroyed our hunting and gathering lifestyle.

The mission period lasted from 1769 to 1840. During the Mission period, 150,000 California indigenous people lost their lives. Many Tataviam people died at the mission. This was due to the enslavement of indigenous people at the missions. Colonists forced the tribal people at the missions to work long hours in inhumane conditions, including children as young as six years old. They were fed very little food and were beaten as punishment by priests and soldiers. This weakened our people greatly. In addition, Tataviam people had not had hundreds of years to adjust to various diseases like the Europeans had; they did not have immunity and antibodies. Rather, when indigenous peoples caught the flu, smallpox, measles, chicken pox, or other illnesses, they could not fight off the disease and often died. There were several epidemics as this was a time before vaccines. In addition to the death of our people, the Tataviam had to endure the death of aspects of our culture. We were not allowed to speak our native tongue. We had to learn Spanish, and starting in the 1850s, we had to learn English. We could not read or write our own languages for several decades. Our language was nearly lost. Today, we are working with community members to revitalize our language. Simply put, our traditional way of life was lost due to the ways the Spanish culture saw our culture as either inferior or as a threat. They viewed us as not fully human until the mission baptized us. We were not compensated for our work or our immense knowledge about the land. Our young people learned skills to be workers on ranches or on farms. They did not learn how to hunt or how to gather traditional foods. The young Tataviam did not learn the traditional ways of life; they learned how to be workers for the Spanish and Mexican landowners.

The mission padres had promised the Tataviam people that, if we became Catholics and citizens of Spain, they would give us our land back. So, we did as we were told as an act of survival. Those who disobeyed were severely punished.

When the mission was dismantled, the Mexican government gave most of the land to Spanish settlers and soldiers, but our ancestors also received some. My family petitioned for and received Rancho Encino from the Mexican governor, for example. However, if land was given to any Tataviam people, they were constantly threatened by neighboring and encroaching settlers. If the Tataviam people successfully protected their lands from settlers, they were then charged large taxes and fees under colonial rule, which is problematic when you cannot read or write in the new government's language. The settling governments knew we had no money or English literacy, so the little land granted to us was quickly taken away by politicians and tax collectors.

After the mission period, early California history was also an extremely difficult time for all indigenous tribal people. The destruction of our natural resources continued. Ranching, farming, and construction of hundreds of towns required the removal of millions of oak trees. The removal of native plants for farming also continued to destroy the native resources the Tataviam people had lived on for thousands of years.

No indigenous peoples of California had legal rights when California became a state in 1850. We were not made citizens of the United States of America for another 70 years. That was in 1924. We were labeled savages. We were sold as indentured servants, which is slavery. It is estimated that early settlers took over 27,000 California indigenous people as indentured servants, and over 7,000 were children. I believe the numbers were much higher since we had no legal rights and many abuses of indigenous people were not reported. Brutal state and federal anti-Indian policies and campaigns costing upwards of $1.6 million were responsible for the deaths of thousands of indigenous people during the California genocide. By 1900, the Tataviam people were almost extinct with just a handful of surviving families making up the Fernandeño Tataviam tribe. The few Tataviam people who did survive this awful time went on to become our Tataviam tribe of today. Today, there are more than 1,000 Tataviam people.

Today, the Tataviam people continue to honor our tribal ways. We still live, hunt, gather, do business, and walk on Tataviam land. We are revitalizing our traditional language. We are replanting our native plants. We are passing on traditional ecological knowledge. We are empowering our youth and honoring our elders. We are building our kiic, our traditional houses. We are doing ceremony with our neighboring tribes today like we did for thousands of years: the Chumash, Yuhaviatam, Tongva, Kitanemuk, and Yokut people, to

name a few, are still the neighbors of the Tataviam people. Those
of you reading this book are the neighbors of the Tataviam people.
Indigenous tribal people are an important part of all communities.
All of us walk on indigenous land, tribal land.

We are the First Peoples, Indigenous Americans. I am a proud
member of the Fernandeño Tataviam Band of Mission Indians.

Ichamc oorvavt (ee-chahm-ch or-vavt), "we are strong."

For more history information,
please visit www.tataviam-nsn.us

For more information about
Alan Salazar's educational
programs and story telling please
visit www.mynativestories.com

— Alan Salazar
"Puchuk Ya'ia'c" (Fast Runner)
Tribal Elder

About the
Illustrations

by Mona Lewis

Paint Stones found in Tataviam and Chumash Territories

The illustrations
were made with stones and soil respectfully foraged from within Tataviam and Chumash territories.

Alan and I found many of these paint stones in the Santa Clarita valley, right near the tribal villages of his ancestors. We collected other natural paint materials, including mussel shells, charcoal from the Woolsey fire, and magnetic sands from Malibu and the beaches of southern California, traditional Chumash land.

Willow Charcoal

Mussel Shells (Chumash)

Jalama Beach (Chumash)

Santa Clara River

Ventura (Chumash)

Santa Clara River

Ojai (Chumash)

Ventura (Chumash)

Ventura (Chumash)

Santa Clarita (Tataviam)

Santa Clara River (Tataviam)

Ventura (Chumash)

Chalk (Tataviam)

Harmony (Chumash)

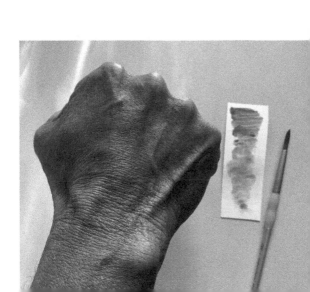

Vivianite
(PNW Lumi Tribe)

The only exception in the collection is the blue vivianite ocher, which I used mostly for the sky tones. It comes from the north shore of Washington state and Vancouver. The vivianite found there formed thousands of years ago as the result of tsunamis that flooded the shoreline, leaving phosphorus and iron to interact and oxidize into the blue ocher you see. The Coast Salish and neighboring tribal people in the Pacific Northwest have used it for thousands of years for painting totem poles.

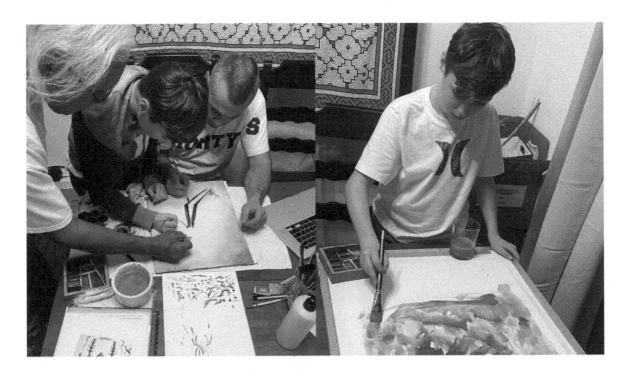

The portrait illustrations in this book feature members of the three families that make up the Tataviam Band of Mission Indians: Alan Salazar on page 15, Destinee Leilani Jimenez (granddaughter of Kathy Ann Flores in the Ortega lineage) on page 23, Caden Salazar on page 24, Ben Cooke on page 27 and Beverly Folkes on page 37.

It is our hope that more tribal artists will take up the work of bringing back these traditional paints. We invited several members of Alan's family to participate in the illustrations for this book. Alan, his children Melissa and Eric, and also his grandson, Caden, all worked on some of the paintings. Hopefully, this is just the beginning.

— Mona Lewis, Illustrator

For more from artist Mona Lewis
visit www.sunspritehandwork.com,
follow @sunspritehandwork
on Instagram and Facebook or email
sunspritehandwork@yahoo.com

Try Making
Pigment
Yourself!

On your next walk around your neighborhood, slow your pace and look carefully in the soil where you live. See if you can find rocks that are soft and have some color. You can test to see if they are soft enough by rubbing them on the back of a tile, or any hard rock near by. If they easily leave a mark, they will be good for pigment.

Next, gently tap your pigment rock with a hammer until it is broken into small pieces. If you have a mortar and pestle, place the pieces in the mortar and grind to a fine powder.

If you don't have a mortar and pestle, grind the small rocks to a powder using circular motions with your hammer. Pour your powdered pigment through a small strainer to sift out the larger pieces. Now your powdered pigment is ready to use!

You may add a little water to this powder and paint with it, but it is easy to make a lovely picture just by rubbing the dry pigment directly on paper. Find instructions to paint you own cave wall handprint painting on page 72.

Find soft, colored stones and break them into pieces

Grind the stone pieces into a fine powder

Store your pigment powders in small containers

Rub dry pigment on paper or mix with water for wet paint

Top: Salazar/Ortega lineage. Bottom right : the family of Kathy Ann Flores, representing the Ortiz line. Bottom left: Cooke/Garcia line. These are the three families that make up the Tataviam Band of Mission Indians.

Make a
Cavewall
Handprint
Painting
Using Earth Pigments

It is easy to make paint by grinding rocks or soil and simply adding a binder. Water, saliva, oil, and eggs are just a few traditional binders. Here's a simple painting you can make using just rocks or soil from your area and water.

Supplies
Soft rocks and soil (some dark and some light)

Sturdy watercolor paper

Water

Paintbrush

Toothbrush

Palette

Scissors

Mortar and pestle

Strainer (optional)

Foraging

Learning how to notice the colors beneath our feet is half the work and half the fun! Take a walk around the local neighborhood, wherever you are. Walk slowly and look carefully. Sometimes patches of colored earth may catch your eye. If so, scoop some up and put them in a container to bring home.

If you see a rock of an interesting color, pick it up and test it. Try drawing with it on a really hard stone or on the sidewalk. Is it soft enough to leave a mark? Does any color come off on your hand? If so, it might be a good candidate for paint. Look for one light color, one dark, one warm, and one cool. Your lightest color for this painting needs to be pretty close to white. (You can grind up white chalkboard chalk if you don't have good white paint stones.)

Grinding

Wear a breathing mask and goggles during grinding and sifting to protect from breathing the fine rock particles. Put a small soft rock in your mortar and pound it with the pestle using an up and down motion. (You can also use a hard rock such as a river stone instead of a pestle for grinding.) As the pieces get smaller, you can use a circular motion with the pestle and grind it until it is a fine powder. You can control how fine you want your paint by deciding how long you will grind it. You can also grind your pigments with a hard river stone on a tile or another hard surface.

Sifting

When your powder is fine, place a spoonful into a tea strainer or a fine sieve and shake it, side to side, over a bowl. You might regrind what is too coarse to go through the sifter and sift it again. If there are really hard particles of sand or silica, discard them as they won't work for this.

Painting

Place a little of each powdered earth pigment on a palette (a plate is fine). Keep your lightest color separate for now.

Using a paintbrush, mix a little water with the darkest powdered pigment and brush it on the watercolor paper. Rinse your brush and paint on your other colors, one at a time, covering the entire paper with earth colors. Have fun with this! There is not a wrong way to do it! Allow the colors to play together on the paper. Layer them if you want.

Allow the paint to dry. This will be your cave wall.

While your cave wall is drying, trace your hand on a separate piece of sturdy paper.

Cut it out. This is now a stencil of your hand!

Place the stencil where you want it on the paper.

Using a toothbrush, mix some water with your lightest pigment. Make this a thick paint.

(In some of the oldest rock art, ancient artists blew paint from their mouths or a straw over their hands to create the handprint. We are using a toothbrush instead.)

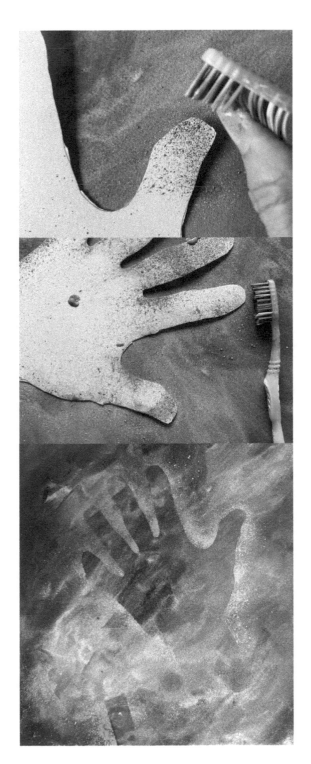

Hold the stencil in place and use the toothbrush to flick dots of white paint all around the edges of your stencil. (Earth pigments usually look darker when they are wet. Don't worry, they will lighten up when they are dry.)

Add more handprints as desired, but be careful to let the white paint dry in-between layers.

You may cut little silhouettes out of the leftover pieces and paint them on in the same way to represent ancestors. You may want to paint the handprints of your whole family!

About the Author
Alan Salazar
"Puchuk 'Ya'ia'c"
(Fast Runner)

Alan Salazar is a traditional storyteller, a native educator, and a native monitor/consultant. He is a tribal elder in both the Fernandeño Tataviam and Ventureño Chumash tribes. He is a tribal spiritual advisor and a traditional paddler of Chumash canoes. His native ancestors were brought into the San Fernando Mission starting in 1799. Like many Fernandeño natives, his family has Tataviam ancestry from the Tataviam village of Chaguayanga near Santa Clarita, California and Tochonanga in present-day Pico Canyon, California. His Chumash ancestry is from the Chumash village of Ta'apu near Simi Valley, California. He continues to actively protect his ancestor's village sites and tribal territories.

Alan has been actively involved with several native indigenous groups. He is a founding member of the Kern County Native American Heritage Preservation Council, Chumash Maritime Association, and a member of the California Indian Advisory Council for the Santa Barbara Museum of Natural History, a community advisor with the Ventura County Indian Education Consortium for over 25 years, and is currently active on the Elder's Council for the Fernandeño Tataviam Band of Mission Indians.

As a member of the Chumash Maritime Association, Alan helped build the first working traditional Chumash plank canoe (tomol) in modern times, and has paddled in plank canoes for over 22 years.

The Chumash of antiquity used their tomols to travel extensively between the California coast and the Channel Islands. They had villages on each of the islands, and friends and families traveled inter-island to fish, visit and trade. Alan is one the most experienced Chumash paddlers in modern times, participating in every modern re-enactment of the crossings starting from Oxnard to Santa Cruz Island.

Alan has also been involved with teaching youths about native American cultures for over 25 years. He has created educational programs at schools, museums and cultural events both in the United States and in Great Britain.

As a spiritual adviser within the Fernandeño Tataviam and Chumash communities, Alan leads ceremonies and prayer circles during traditional native indigenous gatherings. He was raised to be proud of his native indigenous heritage and takes pride in being a positive role model and a respected elder.

This book is an original story that Alan wrote in the spirit of Tataviam storytelling. It is his sincere hope that you will enjoy it and learn something about this beautiful land.

About the Illustrator
Mona Lewis

Mona's family comes from the United Kingdom, France, and Scandinavia. She is a watercolor artist and teacher of handwork in Waldorf education since 1996. She is co-director of the Waldorf Practical Arts Teacher Training program associated with the Southern California Waldorf Teacher Training Institute. Mona trains artists, teachers and home-schooling families in the plant-dye arts and in the practical arts of the Waldorf curriculum.

Using traditional historical dye plants such as indigo, madder, and weld, as well as local indigenous dye plants such as black walnut and costal sagebrush, she created a plant dye garden on the campus at Highland Hall Waldorf School. Students from Kindergarten through the 12th grade participate in caring for the garden from seed to harvest. Using these plants to dye fibers for their handwork projects, students learn about the cultures in which these dye plants originate through hands-on experience of these ancient cultural arts.

Mona is the author of *Nature's Paintbox: Colors from the Natural World for the Young Artist (and Those Who Are Young at Heart)*, released in 2021, and has illustrated two books for Alan Salazar, this one and also *Tata, the Tataviam Towhee, a Tribal Story*.

All three books are available at www.sunspritehandwork.com.

Through feather
        and blade, on petal
and soft breezes,
        these stories still flow
through the land,
        inviting us to listen . . .
for now we are
        a part of it too.